NATIONAL GEOGRAPHIC

What Lives in a Swamp?

Jacob Fink

Frogs live in a swamp.

Bugs live in a swamp.

Snakes live in a swamp.

Fish live in a swamp.

Turtles live in a swamp.

Birds live in a swamp.

What else lives in a swamp?

NATIONAL GEOGRAPHIC

Windows on Literacy®

Science Titles • Emergent Level • Set A

A Bird Flies By
Hot and Cold
Living Things Need Water
Look at the Tree
Making a Hat
Making Raisins
My Bed Is Soft
People Build Dams
Some Things Float
The Baby Shark
The Little Panda
This Is an Island
Toys
Watch the Sky
Weather in the City
What Can a Diver See?
What Lives in a Swamp?
When the Rain Comes
Wood
You Can Make a Pom-Pom

Picture Credits:
Cover, 3, NHPA/ANT Photo Library; 1, 2, 6, 7, 8, Raymond K. Gehman/NGS Image Collection; 4, back cover, Chris Johns/NGS Image Collection; 5, George Grall/NGS Image Collection.

Written by Jacob Fink

2017 2016 2015
9 8 7 6 5 4 3

Published by National Geographic Society,
Washington, D.C. 20036

Windows on Literacy program developed by
Barrie Publishing Pty Limited and Gilt Edge Publishing

ISBN: 978-0-7922-8657-8
Printed in China (CTPS/03)

Think and Discuss

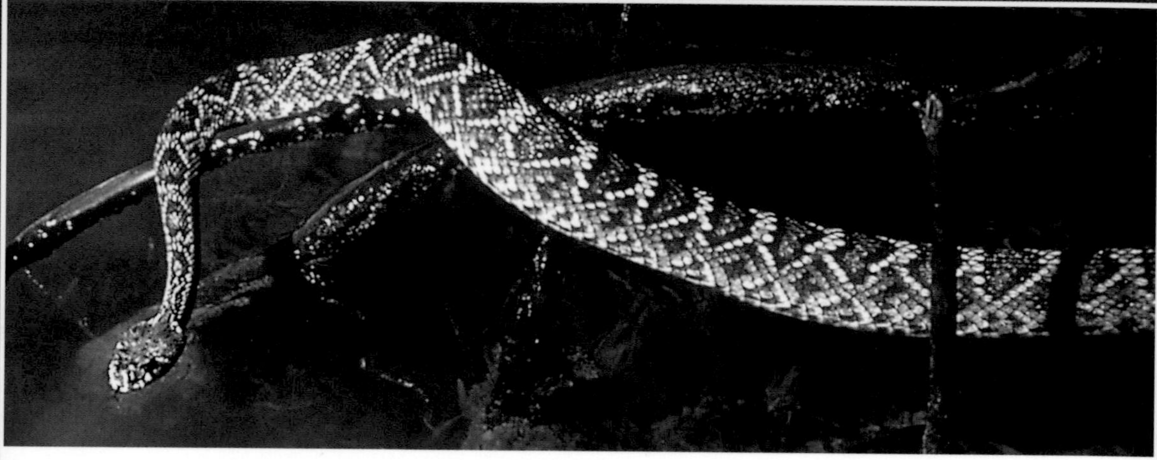

Where else do snakes live?

NATIONAL GEOGRAPHIC
School Publishing

Step Up | Emergent | Early | Fluent | Fluent Plus

1 · · · 13 · · · 24

Science • Set A

ISBN: 978-0-7922-8657-8

NATIONAL GEOGRAPHIC

Windows on Literacy®

School Today and Long Ago

Mario Lucca

Teaching Notes

Early–Level 11

Literacy Focus

Word Count and Vocabulary
- Word Count: 110 words
- High Frequency Words: *my, this, went, when*
- Content Words: *great, grandpa, school, classroom, desk, chalk, slate, pencil, paper*

Decoding Skills
- Initial Consonant Blends: *wr, gr (wrote, write, great, grandpa)*
- Vowel Digraph: *oo (school, book, wooden, too, classroom, looked)*
- Short Vowel Sounds: *i, a (sit, this, sat)*

Comprehension/Thinking Skills
- Stating a purpose for reading
- Using illustrations to make predictions about text
- Comparing and contrasting

Writing/Speaking and Listening
- Writing words in a crossword puzzle
- Sharing ideas about living long ago
- Answering questions about the text

Social Studies Focus

Content and Thinking Skills
- Learning that things change over time
- Understanding that some things stay the same
- Describing how schools and learning have changed over time
- Comparing and contrasting schools now with schools long ago

Building Social Studies Background
This book compares schooling today to the schooling of long ago. Using old photographs as a source of information, it demonstrates some of the changes that have occurred over time, but it also shows that some things remain the same. Some of the ideas covered in the text are changes in classrooms, school equipment, and writing materials.

For more detailed notes and assessment options, see the Teacher's Guide or use our online guide at www.NGS.com